THE WORLD IN PLACE OF ITSELF

THE WORLD
IN PLACE
OF ITSELF

Bill Rasmovicz

ALICE JAMES BOOKS
FARMINGTON, ME

10 9 8 7 6 5 4 3 2 1

Alice James Books are published by Alice James Poetry Cooperative, Inc.,
an affiliate of the University of Maine at Farmington.

Alice James Books
238 Main Street
Farmington, ME 04938

www.alicejamesbooks.org

Library of Congress Cataloging-in-Publication Data

Rasmovicz, Bill, 1970–
The world in place of itself / Bill Rasmovicz.
p. cm.
ISBN-13: 978-1-882295-64-7
ISBN-10: 1-882295-64-1
I. Title.

PS3618.A77W67 2007
811.6—dc22
2007022250

Alice James Books gratefully acknowledges support from
the University of Maine at Farmington and
the National Endowment
for the Arts. ❧

Cover Art: ©Stockbyte Photography
veer.com

CONTENTS

III

IV

V

ACKNOWLEDGMENTS

Grateful acknowledgment is made to the editors of the following journals in which these poems, some in earlier versions, first appeared:

Ellipsis: "Transpiring"
Euphony: "I Tried to Find My Way Back to the Living"
Gulf Coast: "The Myth of Ourselves,"
   "Ballad of the Never Believers"
Hotel Amerika: "Floating," "Giant's Despair"
Mid-American Review: "Crows"
Nimrod: "Tidal"
Poetry Miscellany: "All the Years," "Construction Work,"
   "My Poland"
Puerto del Sol: "Transcendence"
Terra Incognita: "Aberrations I"
The Café Review: "Portrait of the Man Trying to Shed Enough
   Mass to Fly," "Night Courier"
The Comstock Review: "On Becoming Light"
Third Coast: "The Accordion"

The spirit, like everything else, has been trembling

—RENE CHAR

CROWS

Anvils in overcoats.
Battery acid come alive.

Whatever I think of them, they hear
and drag the garbage cans into the street,
flood the cellar with rain.

This morning, one wants the crumpled fruit
of our Japanese cherry. It watches me
watch it, my hands around the throat of a coffee cup.

. . . .

The knit of its wings tight as Kevlar,
its acetylene gaze and butcher block eyes: who,
I have to wonder, is watching whom?

. . . .

That any sound escapes the barbs of their beaks.
I wonder what other arsenal is held
in the hulls of their throats.

They hang on the wires, soldiers
awaiting instruction.

They preen the highway of its waste for a world
made to look our own.

. . . .

At 5:00 A.M. I wake to their cacophonous debates
on how many of them
it would take to lift the steeple

from the church, to pick the constellations clean.
One, I've recently heard trying to mimic the sound
of a chicken next door.

. . . .

Sleet or heat, they persevere.
I talk low when they're near, or not at all.

. . . .

What they want are more gravestones to topple,
frost to whet their blighted voices.

They'd have me believe my bones
were exhumed from the rubble of Warsaw,
that I was assembled from a nest of razor wire.

At night I hear them prying nails from the floorboards
with the grappling hooks of their feet,
dragging our house god knows where.

. . . .

How simple it would be: a stone or a stick,
a trace of arsenic in the trash.
Who would know?

. . . .

They dance around their dead like gypsies
at their children's wedding,
their wings flailing like umbrellas blown inside out.

They traipse through the yard, broken wheelbarrows
bribed to walk.

. . . .

Is it that the sun were a blister ready to pop?

That my life were magnesium powder drizzled
over flame?

In the afternoons, I listen for their shadows
swallowing the room.

. . . .

Their nest, I believe, is in the neighbor's coal bin.
I angle the blinds so they can't see in.

. . . .

I've changed the locks.
I breathe as lightly as possible.

THE MYTH OF OURSELVES

We are all blood relatives to murderers
and cons or victims and thieves.
Even the body seems scarcely a home
with its hollow streets,
its withered facades and nervous citizenry.

We own nothing of ourselves:
the knickknack and ramshackle assemblages
of memory, our children, our scars
or this feeling of hard earth beneath us.

Because this life is never enough, we invent faith
for the sake of rescue, rescue
for the sake of becoming
something we could never be.

All this we live with: that even in its gentleness
the wind may devour us,
that in love, there is somehow the lack of it.
Or that everything might be so much of nothing:

plumes of smoke dissolving, entire lives
constructed of mirrors and wires
and this great illusion of time
where each moment is a desperate bartering

for the next, that there may be
an even greater happiness
here, where we reside
on the brink of losing everything,
of becoming exactly ourselves.

FLOATING

Of all skies, the one tearing the ground
from itself.

Dusk, my pulse in my teeth.
A single boat hauling in the darkness.

What is it that devours us?
Upright from the tide, the head of a monkfish,
its eyes eaten out.
From the shipyard, steam

where they're manufacturing the hour
from sludge and steel.

Somewhere our lives are beginning again
without us.

Of all substance, is it the body
closest to light? Is it silence, the amplitude
of unrest?

The scrawl of gulls and lolling mist,
I hold my breath,
a weight to keep me from rising.

ALL NIGHT THE RAIN

Not from pagodas of charred cumuli, but a flatiron
of humidity. This could be me:
the road dissolving at each end in mist,
the gate peeled back like a broken rudder.

Slugs pilgrimage to the sidewalks.
The pavement percolates with dull sparks.
The tincture of earth tattoos the air and I swear
the living room tastes like a root cellar.
Heavy with itself, my consciousness collapses.

My thoughts blur like wet newspaper.
Still there is a man walking his dog in the alleyway,
swimming through a television full of static.

All night pennies pound the rooftops.
All night the house floats like a stone guitar
and I drift in and out of sleep, swells of sparse traffic
lapping at the windowsill.

Poppies dance in a snake charmer's trance
and I wonder if I'll ever hear the timbre
of sun-crumpled leaves again.

Until I'm jolted awake to find my wife
gone and I see through the rippled window
where the house has come to rest: gulls
piercing the dawn, mist rising on what new world?

BALLAD OF THE NEVER BELIEVERS

I cannot imagine Molotov sunsets
or the inaudible riotousness of foxgloves, tiger lilies,
or the red dew-licked poppies bugling
at the flint strike of dawn.

I have no need for a steepletop honed
to a splintering shine by a bloodshot harvest moon.

My heart is not a glacier slowly melting,
a sorrowful heap of tombstone rubble,
or a matchbox ship without oars.

Nor is the landscape of my mind
a desolate factory yard consecrated
by bullet casings and chemical spill.

I have never wakened to the marauding unrest of crows
or been entranced by the ferment
of yellow lamplight, or strayed
into the mythical wilderness of unending fog.

I do not believe my days are constructed
by an ancient blueprint of the stars.
Not once have I discovered at the foot of my door
a throbbing, anonymously delivered pair of cherub wings.

And I have never known the night to shatter
like a porcelain doll dropped
from a train trestle at the arrival of midnight.

The skin of an onion has nothing to do with the moon.
A liquidambar leaf
in flames has nothing to do with forever.

LADDER

Noticed more now for not being there,
it lay against the house, a repository
of nails and screws, half buried in gravel,
half woven through the overgrown yew.

So who would have stolen it, meaning why—
that splinter trap, sculpture of attrition, bonfire wood?
And when? Surely not in the afternoon,
down the daylight theater of the sidewalk, peripheral
to the woman tending garden two houses over.

In the hour adjacent to dawn,
when even the gate's slightest noncompliance
would be most heard for it being quiet outside?

By secrecy of rain or slow burn of streetlamp;
alone or accompliced; in desperation or mischief?
Doesn't desire bribe the mind for its quenching,
the senses always insist on further investigation?

Did they just up and walk away with it
through hum of transformer and fugue of crickets,
past the solitary traffic of the neighbor
wasted on the anguish of a week at factory,
to hoist then against some vacant tenement window
or the telephone wires—the body only doing

what it somehow must—like that boy who scaled
the electrical tower toward his spectral curiosity,
the meager light of knowing? Or to ascend where?

RULES FOR A SEMI-AUSPICIOUS LIFE

Never cross your arms like a dead man's. Never remove
the crucifix above your bed. Never think of your skeleton
as flotsam or a fossil with a lease for walking. Never believe
your eyes were meant for anything but car crashes, temptation,
ruin. Never hail yourself the sole inhabitant of your body.
Never think your throat a mine shaft you might fall into
or assume your words were meant for anything but
gasoline and a match. Never hold your breath too long.
Never furnish a razor your name. Never clean your rifle at the
kitchen table. Never stare at the doll whose eyes were chewed
out by the dog. Never let the grass swallow the gravestone.
Never wager your teeth. Never hide in the coal cellar. Never
talk in your sleep. Never believe the one who answers.

NASCENT

Random things: the gurgle of roots being torn,
perfume of creosote, of a neighborhood burning

so it is only now that you consider
the nest above your door
you weren't supposed to have removed,

the saint shrunken in her display by the desiccant
of all those years you mistook as separation
between was and is.

Having breathed the murk of the pond's water
while the rest were at picnic, you think now
you should know something.

About the infant in her plastic chamber, nurtured
by the truant pulse of red light, about the children
on their trampoline the sky keeps turning away,

of subterfuge and seraphim,
flood your first memory, *hot* your first word.

TIDAL

How the leaves achieve their scintillation I don't know.
Or the sun its valiant suicide.

That so often it is unnoticeable, there in the pulsating mist,
down in the moonglow,
in the tenor of crows and inebriating dolor of night.
What I own least is my heart.

That I can recall my brother's face at all, how else
could I say I love you or these days falling through me,
a stone falling through honey?

And all in a single breath: bio-luminescence
threshing the shore and eons concealed in a passing cloud.

Is it death that lingers as beauty in the tendrils of the flower,
where the fire, dwindled, comes back again

rampant? At the confluence of this wind
rattling the gutters, the sun nearly gone and hour ready?

ASSIMILATION

My ancestors cheated even the grave.
About my brother, I can only remember how blue he was.
A castle on the cliff
and the people are happy.

The cars trundling by, the city with its eyes torn out—
I can still hear the hour from which we were born
sobbing in the dark.

Na zdravje, then! Here's to climbing the fire escape
while the building burns, to the assimilation of a knife
for a tongue.
Should I float off, or sink? Should I ignite?

Forgive me! I'm speaking from all fours, my skull's echoing
like a looted tabernacle:
another psalm for the dead.
I'd like to offer now these blistered roses,
these cellophane tears.

How long does it take to lose the taste of what's lost?
Quick! Your sharp eye, and thread for suture.

WHERE I COME FROM

Most afternoons the moon pirouettes above us
like an ostrich egg balanced on the tip
of a sewing needle.
But sometimes, in the summertime,
the sun just fills right up to bursting

and the petals of our yellow rosebush
become butterfly wings, and butterflies fill the sky
like a yellow rain rising upward
so that you can hardly see.

Every day the past gets wheeled around
on a squeaky steel gurney, and every day
the same melted-candle-faced man goes to work
inside the imbroglio of the town clock,
grinding down the knife edge of years.

Everyone knows everybody else
and the houses line the avenues like soldier ants
against a terminally encroaching buttery sunset.
The clouds float by like magnifying glasses
and no one speaks of the night that follows.

SOPRA VOCE

You are correct to assume that your incessant pacing
will not precipitate speech from the floorboards.
You are your own dispossessed muse.

You must know that your crumpled pages do not morph
into the fists of tyrants. Your words

are not a process of fusion, alchemy, or siphoning the virgin
luminosities of fireflies. Nor are they reliquaries,
or requiems for that which they stand.

Certain things to consider:

the thing itself as myth, "voice" as learning to speak
the way you already speak.
On the subject of love, why do you amble about
like a horse on stilts, then run on about death like a gutter

full of rain water? Why not joke?
Why so fascinated by the dead?
Must the laminations of memory coalesce
into the inextractable compendium of your being?

Remember the shopkeeper's smile of scattered nails,
or the crows conducting their daily audit of your whereabouts
from the front lawn.

Forget what you know. Know what you fear—
for what does desire or grief have you erupt?
Discard your rubbing stone and perfunctory contritions.

How could anything but real dread or joy prompt you
to saying?

You must agree to the terms and conditions
of never knowing, learn
not to pull so quickly your burning hand from the fire.

Pretend you are more humble than you are.
Pretend you are a god, that words
don't matter,
that they are everything.

ABERRATIONS I

In photographs I appear drugged, weightless;
my eyes are sirens.

In my dreams there are no horses or pearled moons,
everyone is missing and I'm looking for them.
I get tired of so many sanctimonious horizons,

operations, birthdays and funerals.
Even at rest, I feel dizzy all the time.

At night, I can hear the turbines of the years ushering
me off while opossums dismantle the garbage.

I am frightened and I am comforted.
Mornings, I am assaulted by loneliness;

evenings, the pheromones of dusk.
I know the dead are right here listening.

I know words adhere to nothing.
I am studying the density at which the heart collapses,

a stone evaporates.
Already my hands are the weathered feet of a crow,

my voice, dogs rummaging through bones.
My clothes are smoke.

I shiver at the hours lining up
then falling away like parishioners at communion,

and the children asleep in their tiny rooms,
curled tight as fists.

NIGHT COURIER

I can hear your rusty chain, your creaky bearings,
the metronome of your bent rim.
I can hear you thumping your message
up and down the street against everyone's screen door.
I've seen your tire tracks in the flower beds.
You cannot hide beneath your hat yanked down over
your eyes, your coat pulled up over your nose.
One day your pant leg will get caught in the sprocket
and you'll go over the handlebars.
One day you will find your bicycle and bag hanging
from the telephone wires.
The rain does not deter you, you've tempered the wind.
You've been at it for years now.
Who is it you are working for?
I can see morning's horizon like the glow
of the penitentiary; you've got the whole planet in tow,
and not a grunt or a groan.
You never come around for the money, you never stop
for a breath or a smoke, you never look tired.
I am on to you.

MY POLAND

By its scent, it is ash and creosote, skin
of the accordion.

It's the bowels of a cellar dug by hand
in which your clothes are hung to dry, to reek of soot
and nails and years ago.

The way the tiny gravestone floats like a suitcase in the grass
up there on the hill.

It's your bleached-cork complexion,
the notch in your brow like the bend in the Carpathians
where they escape southward at the border.

The gold ring around your mother's tooth;
a tiny halo holding her up.

The boiling of pig's feet and duck's blood.
Rosaries stuffed in the back of the nightstand;
muffled prayers reciting themselves ad infinitum
for the dog to shut up, for the pipes to unfreeze,
for the penance of living.

Sermon drone, hymns where the choir
sang as though with their mouths full of meat, a language
you never learned.

The quarantine of photographs cradling each other,
like hands clenching for a morsel of food, a drop
of wine, or water.

Its eloquently brooding cities and lugubrious black rivers,
rivers of sulfur, anorexic rivers; mirror-less,

scars in motion, distilled
through your gray namelessness.

Where you know the weather by the hinge of your ankles,
and where news is always who married whom
or whose chest erupted during an eclipse of dreaming.

Where the stutter of the streetlight
beneath the gasoline-soaked rag of the sky
illumines the mutt scouring the alleys for the garbage.

Its electrical towers, false obelisks,
its wires and tubes siphoning afternoons,
then spitting them out.

And the splatter of scree for landscape.
And the green fire of the leaves,
and house lights staying on late for hardly anyone sleeping.

It's the crutches, the couch, the cigarette burns
and loss of people to things, the left-over screws
and flammables too close to the furnace.

The ants hemorrhaging from wood,
the tempest of feathers the hawk leaves beneath the vines.

It's the mouth subjected to its tongue.
Knowing the body by its breaking.
It's laughing daily at the bit of dying you do.

ARS METAPHYSICA

Your head is a landscape revised by culm
and tire smoke, you stare through the window
as though words will appear,
heraldic and from nowhere.

Light as a paper bag, you amble about town
waiting for the wind to take hold.
You profess the body is a cello, and the moon
the eye by which you see.

You maintain your ancestors were barbarians,
that the tongue can out-leverage a crowbar.
You ascertain the weather with a fork
and an empty bottle of port.

Moths sleep under the mattresses of your eyelids.
You testify to wolves inhabiting your bones at night.
You claim the dead speak through you.

Crows circle your house like tiny hurricanes.
Saplings take root in your gutters.
Your own voice frightens you.
You're a liar, a thief. You're vain.

You believe you can extract silence from a stone.
You contend the friction between pen and paper
creates light. You believe the darkness
is larger than any space can hold.

NOCTURNE

The islands
removed from their installations.

Below the window, a dog pissing in the street.

Tangential voices.
Then, the flash of a gull like a severed rope:

the basilica under the weight of itself.

Me. Here.
Waiting for the light to begin.

I WOKE FROM PARTIAL SLEEP

I woke from partial sleep: sirens, or a baby
falling past my window.
The refrigerator humming like an elevator abruptly stopped.

I stumbled through the hallway
into silence. Oddly, I could hear myself listening,
breath inflating, contracting the room.

Wind pulsed the air like notes from a drowning piano,
and with the warm odor of laundry,
other lives wrapping around me.

I put my hand to the wall; behind it, the sea, and a vibration
like electricity from the earth.
I slipped on the wooden floor in my socks,

and in one giant gulp, a rush then
of black sand pouring through me. I could see myself
from the bottom of a hollow skyscraper.

Below me, layers of blue compounding into black.
Nowhere was there bottom.
Then, a night bird's sounds of query, a moth

at the porch light abducting its shadow.
I could feel myself evaporating. Each utterance I conceived
dripped from the telephone wires,

my fear thumping the air like a fog light,
the clothes hung out to dry in the glistening dark,
a stone holding its breath.

AFTER THE APOCALYPSE

Outside, children were laughing, their glowing voices
modulating toward dark.
The quiet hunched over us, pressing on the roofs,
and without our having lost anything, there was loss.
The parked cars we saw now as old war machines.

Calamity's only real evidence, a wet newspaper
glued to the street wind or flame could not unpeel.
What precisely had ended?
Not the dog dragging its chain, not the trash lined
curbside or the telephone wires
drawing off the last filaments of daylight.

With little designed for the architecture of words,
eventually, we returned to our voices to say things like,
that was close or *so much for the trumpets and stampede,*
then kissed or watched TV.

Inside the grocery store we shared condolences
with the manager of perishables and cashier,
for the past, for the future we knew we'd screw up.

Forever came and went, the trees only slightly bent.
Somehow we'd have to look forward again
to the glimmer of morning's fatigue churning the leaves,

as it appeared we were left only with ourselves,
and the awful proximity of now.

GIANT'S DESPAIR

I stepped outside myself
in the effluvium of passers-by.
My life, in spite of all I loved, was

rainwater skidding into a sewer grate.
The withered sack of a man retrieving
his groceries from the cobblestones,

the mildew of city lights, a distortion
of souls. That I could stand here at all—
the desire of my cells to be dust,

pigeons scattering from a windowsill.
I checked my pocket for a wallet,
keys. I wanted to believe I was more

than the speculation of a few stars.
I was free, but of what?
Dusk was stealing the sheen from

a lapidary's window, the stray rim
of a bicycle, scrunching itself into a fist.
I reached to recover myself.

My tongue swelled fat as a loaf
of bread. Slack then, the night unmoored
from its iron post, and all around me

the buildings sagging, my lungs heaving
from the weight of god.
Or his absence.

ALL THE YEARS

It was late—or very early.
The dark was palpitating in the lilacs.
I turned on the light, rose from bed,
paced the room, retired, and got up again.

A star was drooling in the corner of the window.
I was writing it all down—
the house was a pendulum: nearer, further,
then nearer again to the sea.

All the years of my life gathered in the yard to graze.
I yelled up from the mineshaft of my throat.
No one could help.
There was my mother's blue coat,

and the air was perfumed with bologna sandwiches.
The other houses were asleep.
Steam rose from the nostrils of a manhole cover.
I felt sad and alone.

Then happy.
There was only the world.
An invisible and inevitable mass was filling me.
Deer were snorting in the woods.

I was full—a nervous calm.
A small planet was prying at my chest.
I could taste myself shivering.
I steadied myself in the doorway, and the floor fell away.

Silence unfurled its wings.
I stood there in the dark, afraid of who I was.
I was not writing these words.
They were writing me.

MAPPING THE ABYSS

Night's flagellum, these trees. Without points of reference,
any measurements of how long or far

only complicate us. The gargle of an exhaust pipe
rattles the window. That, I hear. It is myself
I have to convince myself of.

The rustle of lovers just beyond the wall
like a city of glass no one
is allowed to enter. Scatterings of papers, meaning

obligations, outlines of diminishment.
Even sitting up from the table is a departure:
how speaking entails not speaking.

Still, desire continues
hauling the broken cello of its body forward, the aftertaste

of so many afternoons extinguished
like a match on our tongues.
We listen to the hours seep from us,

afraid that in this history of believing, our hunger
has turned to eye itself.

ABERRATIONS II

I owe everything to the anger making
my body hot, the stray tentacle of light coaxing open

the door. I never believed I would one day glimpse myself
in the tundra of this severed moon.
Or wake with the temperature at which the neighbor
incinerates his leaves.

Now I consider the broken murmur of the river
solace, these downed trees

a means to see. And if anything, I have maintained
reverence for the monotony of blackbirds

disfiguring the lawn, midnights steeped in chloroform
and forgetting. How often I have lived

in place of myself, in a room sworn only to the harboring
of feral twilight
with nothing more than a scalpel, a clock.

And I have loved them anyway: the woman selling
her sex at the cemetery entrance, the bell
that too often summons these pale disaffections,

even if these alleyways to nowhere, these drowned
streets, are merely the city of myself.

ST. PETER ON BEHALF OF THE POET
TO THE TRIBUNAL OF HEAVENLY IMPASSE

Mostly he swallowed his pain.
In his youth he sang a few times at mass, shy as he was
of his own voice.
Ever loathe to describe himself, he believed in the hereafter
to the extent his hands assumed the task of balloons
always carrying him elsewhere.

He assisted an old man once to locate his teeth
in the street where he'd fallen.
He thought it somehow flattering that his collar bones
were crow bars trying to pry him from himself.

He was grateful
for the gulls plummeting through his window
into what might have been nothing.
He was an ark of sorts, ferrying his fractured intuitions
on love and its sentries.

True, his obsession for words often overwhelmed him
(his own voice he continually heard as someone else's),
still he did not mistake them for people, for living.
He stood at the pulpit of his doubt and enunciated for all
his most illusory and private concerns.

His eyes always remained pulpy with rapture.
Which is to say he regarded even a mattress floating
downstream a missed opportunity.

He never ceased to rememeber the bluebird he shot
and dreamt that color of dawn would one day devour him.
Though he fashioned his existence a piano hung
from a fishhook, he admits
it was always more fragile than that.

PORTRAIT OF THE MAN TRYING
TO SHED ENOUGH MASS TO FLY

His wife died too young.
Though long after death, his body went on living.
Every day the same black drapes for pants,
bleached t-shirt.

Atrophied, too heavy for himself,
he sat outside coaxing mine-dust from his lungs,
or else with a tumbler of vodka, gaze fixed
on the constellation of cigarette burns in the kitchen floor.

He spoke only to curse the blackbirds
from the cherry.
He was bruised neck-to-ankle from falling,
his elbows and knees swollen shut where the healing itself
became disease,
though his heart was deemed healthy.

From behind, you could see the outline of his ribs, wings
skin had grown over.
He never ate or slept. His eyes always teared.

By the end, he was nothing more
than the feather left from a sheet of burnt paper.
Which is what would happen if an angel chose flesh.

IV

THE WORLD IN PLACE OF ITSELF

The pressure coiled in my ears, I'd wake:
only trampled grass outside where the hoists and pulleys
were dragged away.

A steepletop prodded the sky to bursting,
though somehow the air was filled again with air.
The light at once arriving and having

always been, these were mornings after which the crows
had their long conversations with the dead
and silence could not be heard for its breaking.

At 8:00 a.m., a man floated by on the scent of his newspaper's
promise and perils.
I could hardly believe the scaffolding of my bones

would hold, how my blood seized
and began again, seamless. Neighbors spoke shruggingly
and if there was talk of love

there was talk of war. Leaves taunted the wind
for more wind, and the sea, gnawed free of the moon,
flapped at the listless shore, resolute with going nowhere.

While through to each follicle,
the sensation: not desire, but a desire for desire,
and hardly even that.

ABERRATIONS III

The stricture of the house in the cold—
only the crows are fat. On the table,

the way a hair splits the light: one minute,
utter buoyancy. Then one's life

as the distillates of the hour set aflame.
How easily the afternoon could give: a certain

gravity living must succumb to, without
our knowing; the neighbor brooming about

the sidewalk talking to the bricks;
the turbulence of dogs dragging their chains.

What tethers us to consciousness?
The quarantined orange in its black bowl,

The sky outside with its surgical sheen.
Is it the body buried inside itself

from which we never emerge? These words,
escapees from solitary confinement

in the prison guard's clothes?
My lungs are evaporating even as we speak.

NO ONE LIVES HERE

No one lives here.
The kitchen table is fastened by the weight of an ashtray.
Soon, even the silence will disappear.

Blackbirds no longer perch in the cherry tree and stare.
Windows that saw with blinding sight have fallen gray.
No one lives here:

the faint radio through the walls, we no longer hear.
The clothes will be discarded, the furniture sold today.
Soon, even the silence will disappear.

The vodka on the counter lies still and clear.
Sunday palms bow the frail doorway.
No one lives here:

the whole house, hanging from the chandelier,
will pendulum tonight and sway,
but soon, the silence will disappear.

Soon the entire house will collapse, razed by the years,
the neighbors have no words to say;
no one lives here.
Even the silence disappears.

THE ACCORDION

Its abbreviated keys, the half-smile one offers
for photographs.
Its music, the whispering of the rosary,
the head of a cabbage split in two.

It prophesizes
that you're bound to cave through the cellar steps,
that at any moment the ambulance outside
might combust.

Its denuded voice of alcohol and cigarettes tells
the same orphaned story of not knowing on what boat,
in whose hands it arrived.

It recalls in its wails picking your grandfather up
from the snow, drunk, his too-big pants at his knees;
the aunt who eventually hoped to see
with her prosthetic eye.

It says it is the everyday that haunts:
the catatonic orchestration of the clothesline leading
the wind, the cat crossing the yard
as though the afternoons were nothing but straight down.

A relic, a symbol for what doesn't work anymore—
this emergency lung stowed in its bomb-proof case
at the bottom of the closet, smelling of cattle, or brine.

Who even knows how to play it?—
its emphysemic wheeze like a plane going down.

It makes us believe that one should be grateful just for
skin, that it contains us.

It dreams of a Sunday someone will finger its dirty teeth
with a polka.

Here on my lap, breath drawn, it longs to sing
of the children found blue in their cribs, this lightless
northern light.

It says it will outlive all of us, and that nowhere
despite our toasts heavenward, does the afterlife exist.

ABERRATIONS IV

Asleep, I don't feel the grinding of my teeth.

A constant tremble occupies my hands.

How often I find myself numb
from the anesthesia of afternoons dissipating,

mistake my breath for the footsteps of children,
frantic in the dusk-burned streets.

The evenings smell of tar, methane.

I am convinced that once unconscious,
I will not wake from the dentist's chair.

I feel cold all the time, disenchanted by the drone
of cicadas and city lights

feigning an ordered cosmology.

My eyelids twitch like the suicides of moths
diving into streetlights.

Death, I know, can be this instant, my jaw,
the hinge of the cellar door.

I pace through my house nervous for words—

the accident from my window, its smoke
a whisper of acid.

RIFT

It is for nothing that I have stood here
in the gaunt light of dusk, passing hours to the refrain
of waves.

Why I have desired a life outside my own I do not know.
These clothes, these words, they are not me.
They bring me no closer to life than to death.

If only to remember a car on the roadside burning
or the fuselage of a cone flower smoldering in neon dusk.

And to think we can love as easily: rise like fiddleheads
toward the impulse of our thirst,
where even in love, one is alone and the small lives
we gather to sing about pulse,

pulse and are gone.
Is it from light born of light that these houses gleam
with the lucidity of a fever? The phosphor of the bone?

Watching the clouds
fracture into clouds, I grow apart from myself.

TRANSCENDENCE

I don't sleep, I listen:
at the far end of the room, the bed suspended by
an incantation.
Outstretched on it, I reach from wall to wall.
The ceiling, high enough
to convince its guests ascension were possible.

In the building opposite, men hunch
at their drafting tables exacting which way an umbrella
will blow through the street later and come to rest,
a snarled bird.

On the end-table:
money, toothpaste, tickets for the trip.

I compare the lines in my hands to cracks in the plaster.
I search for a face in its blemishes, wait for a voice.

Outside, the streetlamp conducts its pale investigation:
graffiti where no one can reach,
someone scouring the dumpster
with the instrumentation reserved for picking a lock.

Strangers, the hours pass each other with barely
a glance.
It is impossible for me to believe I have loved.
Equally impossible then to believe I have not.

Beneath the window, clothes in a heap.
I stare at the fire escape.
Until now, I'm unaware of my chewing myself.

The night shift over, people are exchanged
for more people, the city's exhalation blows papers
through the room.

Acidity of my own breath. Pins and needles
in my toes.
Low clouds. Hiss of steam. My hands over my chest.

In decibels, light trickles down between the buildings.
Morning pried open with a jackhammer.

CROSSING

And if we keep ascending?
Though I am separate from the pain, awareness in my
ears, my spine.

The flight attendant serving cocktails and dinner
defrays the complexities
of altitude, speed and temperature.

What is 70 degrees below zero?
Ice clouds below, bright sun, its pressure:

under the anesthesia, a woman wilts in her seat,
a baby's ears pop.

In the steady increments of the bloodmuscle, the body
driven down like a spike.
The sound only an echo of itself: weight
without mass. The awkwardness of hands, a tongue.

In such thin air, there is little to hold us.

MASS

My mother slipped me candy as a restraint.
Still I opened the umbrella during sermons,

folded pages of the psalm book
into paper airplanes. I wondered why everything

happened so slowly, as in a trance or dream.
I studied the volumes of dust

filtered through the windows as swarms of light,
wondered if the altar boys ever set the place

on fire, and who got to tug on that sad, sad bell.
I never sang. Or only so softly

no one could hear. I always forgot to kneel
at the quiet parts, but after everyone shook hands,

as heavy as that whole place was
with its hordes of flowers you could hear breathing,

there was buoyancy again. We'd line up
down the center aisle, our bodies suddenly

returned to us; while outside, prostrating itself
in the streets, Sunday's rain.

I TRIED TO FIND MY WAY BACK
TO THE LIVING

Without language or country, I sat on the cold steps
minding the river, secured by a fertile history of lament
and its ornate temple of stone.
At once there was quiet
and the indelible traffic of voices.

People looked at me strangely: I couldn't speak,
ask questions, explain myself.
I kept my distance in the shadow of some monuments
where those with foresight came to spend their last days.

I could see through an archway the sculpted wrath
of a deity robed in the red of sacrifice, the solemn postures
of those entering, leaving.
Pigeons ambled across the rooftops.
Whatever my life was I knew was gone.

Across the water, on its embankment, smoke
from a pyre. A family was gathered.
I couldn't discern even the shape of the body set to flame,
just fire turning over itself inducing more fire.

How desire consumes itself—
and history too: the steps beneath me dissolving,
the sparse flowers periscoping through shade
toward the half-light of heavy overcast.

To feel anything for the living or dead
seemed wasted. I could only go on in spite of myself

tasting soot. The river
moved thickly, but moved all the same.

I knew in my chest the breaths I was taking
had been someone else's. That neither words nor the body
held any asylum. I stood up

and sunk my hands in my pockets for the semblance
of something finite and true, while past the horizon line
of houses, some pigeons burst into flight,
back down into the valley. If that's where it still was.

CONSTRUCTION WORK

Traffic. Pebbles of rain.
A black sash of wind dances in the naked room.

Everywhere the enameled grin of windows
seems to recall someone once loved
now gone.

Lampposts are microscopes for the study
of stray dogs.
Haze builds beneath them: smoke
from the friction of earth against sky.

Lonely and tired, the drunken streets stagger
into darkness. A night that does not end.

I lie in the callus of my bed, steam
clanging in the pipes
where someone's assembling a ladder to the stars.

V

MANIFEST DESTINY

Waking up, my eyes crumbled bricks,
my breathing labored from traipsing all night through

the catacombs of sleep. There were wars going on.
You could see it in the lay of their faces.

Dogs coursed through the streets with their own agenda.
Clothes flagged the alleyways. I too was trying to forget

who I was or wasn't; my focus, the blister forming between
my toes from new sandals, where one might obtain

a cappuccino. Hansom boats lined the pier,
and tourists with new tans brandishing cameras, waiting

for the perfect subtropical sunset. Gardens were
strategically planted at intersections, palms imported,

buildings painted adamant shades of pink and yellow.
There was at least the ambiance of someone trying.

Still, how could one help but wonder what the sea was
muttering behind the afternoon's hazy sheen?

Which receded, wave after truckling wave on the rocks,
and everyone so painfully absorbed in their own role:

the trees, bathers floating on their backs and cars
revving by; all of them, bawdy actors. Stand-ins merely

to make manifest the mind's perambulations,
as even the merest absence is less than can be imagined.

RESUMPTION

By midafternoon, one hardly remembered
the evening extracted from our bodies like a nail
from pressured wood. Geraniums burst from the windowsills.

Gone was the terrible aesthesia of daybreak
like a chest cracked open and pried apart.
No one recognized
the bars over their windows or the stains of war.

Voices took root in the crevices. Between tenements,
the wind surrendered to a woman's
white underwear. Bright as nectarines,
the sun rolled off shopkeeper's awnings

into the streets. I walked through town
over the tired pulse of road, honed by lathes
of immersion and erasure.
Bells hammered down the day

into the gunmetal gauze of dusk.
A man threw seed to his chickens like holy water,
while springing up from the dirt all around me
like tiny islands, the Roman empire.

THE FUTURE AS GLIMPSED
IN THE EYE OF A HORSE

In that caliber of dawn muffled
and lit by fog, the horse had come full bore
from the lower end of the field.

Standing sideways, it pinned me with its stare
to the other side of the fence, which panic
and the arpeggio of hooves drove me
to plunge beneath.

In the convexity of its eye, in that black mirror,
I could see myself: my gun at the ready, my body
rigid with adrenaline.
What if I were to have crossed then into oblivion?

I had fed a horse once from my palm.
In the fat of its gaze, I discerned nothing of its myth
or my own, just silence
and uncertainty's wan, skittish light.

What was the opaque prophecy of its eye to tell?
That the body is born of caprice
and feeble enchantments? That impulse of self
I could not abandon.

It stammered and snorted,
awaiting my move. I shot skyward as it came.
Trees frosted by the early hour shattered.
And as abruptly, the horse recoiled—
back into the obscurity of morning.

As did I, my gun cantilevered in my arm,
my briar scrapes and dud grandeur,
tracing the knots of barbed wire into elsewhere.

ABERRATIONS V

Once, I too wanted to walk outside myself.
Now I wonder who owns the missing tooth of my comb,
why these hieroglyphs for trees.

Leaves scour the parking lot like schizophrenic birds.
In my own house, my footsteps sound like water
dripping underground.

I feel freakish in line at the grocery store, the bank.
I still hold a gross fear of the dark.
And hunting down the arbitrators of loneliness,

I've found no one. I've watched the dead burn, peeled
their soot from my face.
I've rolled the luminosity of a firefly
between my fingers; what feels to me now
like cashmere, silk.

What I remember most is my finger caught in the sprocket,
the clarity of the moment before pain, before thought.

I lie in bed listening to the wind vibrate the lock
like soldiers at the door,
teeth chattering in the cold.

THE PEAR TREE IN THE LACHRYMOSE
CHAMBER OF MEMORY

Its bark: petrified sinew. Its shape, an aching upward,
exhibiting a torsion not palpable
in the gloss and slow congeal of the hourly.

The blackbirds fasten themselves
heavy as doorstops. The air above it, dreams dissociated
from their hosts. Where twilight is the afterglow
of the penitentiary, and the dogs
keep after the ghost of a deer roped from a branch.

Where aircraft pass en route to the far sublime, mute
as the neighbor girl who refuses to speak.

Where father revises with saw and sledge in shadowlight,
and the child gathers the ground's rotting ripe fruit
to dissect, for the gorged jewels of drowned bees.

AFTERMATH

The man on the floor is having a seizure.
The empty pants pockets of his eyes are pulled inside out.

His view, straight up into his skull's dark cathedral.
Immediately the supermarket Muzak evaporates.
Silence pours from the loudspeakers, and the world

on its raft of empty barrels begins to drift.
Angels, we hover: the deli-manager's nervous grip

squishing the cheese; the woman fastening the sack of oranges
to her breast; her children at each leg, staring down
from the precipice of their faces. No one speaks

as we acclimate to our bodies, the sheer from
one moment to the next severing the tether of our voices.

Instinctively, someone secures his tongue with a plastic spoon.
The rest of us keep vigil as the thunderhead of his brain
conducts its incantation, the honeycomb of lights

dripping efflorescence on his forehead.
When the trills in his muscles subside, we peel him

from the linoleum, his eyes powdered with confusion,
his skin the aftermath of an avalanche. The music resumes.
And one by one we dissipate into the aisles,

weightless, particles of light; clenching
the sturdiness of our carts for anything solid in this world.

TRANSPIRING

Because of his limp I noticed him approaching,
a blister from too-tight shoes,
the hulk of his frame coerced into women's attire.
His hair was a sort of landscape-of-Mars orange

and his makeup, fermenting honeydew.
As a woman, he wasn't convincing. Not that gender
was the issue, but it looked painful,
and his struggle, mythic: man against himself,

his gaze fixed to where the sole of his shoe was loose
and stuttering now at the sidewalk.
Heat was rising from the pavement, the humidity
bearing down. He looked up, the gravity of my eyes

drawing his. I looked away—
how can the body feel so much
unlike itself as to believe it is someone else?
Who is it we should have been all along

and what part of our nature is in fact transmutable?
The cars were floating by like clouds.
The clouds, diminishing in the pink light of an August
almost gone. But given that we are all

what we may not have had in mind, who amongst us
hasn't sought refuge outside themselves from
the heart's inclement weather?
Should I say hello? The arc of his posture was a wave

about to break. And who was I to think he was
someone other than himself?
At that moment we passed each other, my voice
a stone in my throat, my throat collapsing into itself.

How do I acquire sympathy for the world,
an understanding of what it is to be you, when
the only way to know you is to be you?
I turned to look; he was small in the distance.

In the artifice of my body, *I* was small.
The pink light was gray. The sound of the cars, gray.
An almost criminal silence.
Then, sadness: I was afraid for us both.

ON BECOMING LIGHT

And there it was, the moth:
a child's hand wrestling itself in the grass.
Delirious, it fumbled its way out
from the black umbrella of a tree,
then landed on the stoop.

A frayed rope of light swung from the porch.
The moon was gorged on the dewy foment
of summer.

I set my hand near. It fluttered into my palm,
its weight no more than breath; its wings,
laments hammered into sheets of dust.

The world stalled on its axis, I could hear
the ocean in my bones, the night
nervous with cicadas from years ago.

It pulsed once toward the brightness:
impossible, that we must love what kills us.
I held my hand high to the light until it flew.

Recent Titles from Alice James Books

Equivocal, Julie Carr
A Thief of Strings, Donald Revell
Take What You Want, Henrietta Goodman
The Glass Age, Cole Swensen
The Case Against Happiness, Jean-Paul Pecqueur
Ruin, Cynthia Cruz
Forth A Raven, Christina Davis
The Pitch, Tom Thompson
Landscapes I & II, Lesle Lewis
Here, Bullet, Brian Turner
The Far Mosque, Kazim Ali
Gloryland, Anne Marie Macari
Polar, Dobby Gibson
Pennyweight Windows: New & Selected Poems, Donald Revell
Matadora, Sarah Gambito
In the Ghost-House Acquainted, Kevin Goodan
The Devotion Field, Claudia Keelan
Into Perfect Spheres Such Holes Are Pierced, Catherine Barnett
Goest, Cole Swensen
Night of a Thousand Blossoms, Frank X. Gaspar
Mister Goodbye Easter Island, Jon Woodward
The Devil's Garden, Adrian Matejka
The Wind, Master Cherry, the Wind, Larissa Szporluk
North True South Bright, Dan Beachy-Quick
My Mojave, Donald Revell
Granted, Mary Szybist
Sails the Wind Left Behind, Alessandra Lynch
Sea Gate, Jocelyn Emerson
An Ordinary Day, Xue Di
The Captain Lands in Paradise, Sarah Manguso
Pity the Bathtub Its Forced Embrace of the Human Form, Matthea Harvey
The Arrival of the Future, B.H. Fairchild
The Art of the Lathe, B.H. Fairchild

Alice James Books has been publishing exclusively poetry since 1973. One of the few presses in the country that is run collectively, the cooperative selects manuscripts for publication through both regional and national annual competitions. New regional authors become active members of the cooperative, participating in the editorial decisions of the press. The press, which historically has placed an emphasis on publishing women poets, was named for Alice James, sister of William and Henry, whose fine journal and gift for writing went unrecognized within her lifetime.

Typeset and Designed by Dede Cummings

Printed by Thomson-Shore
on 50% postconsumer recycled paper
processed chlorine-free